# *THE*
# *TROJAN*
# *WOMEN*

## ~~~ *Euripides* ~

*adapted by*

# JEAN-PAUL SARTRE

*English version by* RONALD DUNCAN

New York      1967

## ALFRED · A · KNOPF

C.1

THIS IS A BORZOI BOOK

PUBLISHED BY ALFRED A. KNOPF, INC.

*Also by* JEAN-PAUL SARTRE

*DRAMA*

THE CONDEMNED OF ALTONA, 1961
　　　(*Les Séquestres d'Altona*)
THE DEVIL AND THE GOOD LORD, and Two Other
　　　Plays, 1960
　　　　　(*Le Diable et le Bon Dieu, Kean, Nekrassov*)
THREE PLAYS, 1949
　　　　　(*Les Mains sales, La Putain respectueuse,*
　　　　　　　*Morts sans sépulture*)
NO EXIT and THE FLIES, 1947
　　　(*Huis Clos and Les Mouches*)

*FICTION*

TROUBLED SLEEP, 1951
　　　(*La Mort dans l'âme*)
THE REPRIEVE, 1947
　　　(*Le Sursis*)
THE AGE OF REASON, 1947
　　　(*L'Âge de raison*)

*NONFICTION*

SEARCH FOR A METHOD, 1963
　　　(*Question de Méthode*)


*These are Borzoi Books,*
*Published in New York by* ALFRED A. KNOPF

# THE TROJAN WOMEN

# INTRODUCTION

Why The Trojan Women? Greek Tragedy is a beauti-
ful monument which we inspect with interest and respect with a scrupulous interpreter by our side. But it
is a ruin where nobody would want to live. Devotees
of classic drama periodically attempt to resuscitate
Aeschylus, Sophocles and Euripides, and present them
in their original style. But we are left feeling remote
from such pious parodies. The reason why we find it
difficult to connect with such productions is that these
plays were inspired by an essentially religious concep-
tion of the world which is now completely strange to
us. Though their language can seduce us, it no longer
convinces us. Our aversion to such revivals is not helped
by the many bad versions of the plays which abound.
And when Jean-Paul Sartre chose to adapt a classic
tragedy for the Théâtre National Populaire, and of all
the tragedies the one which is the most static and the
least theatrical, indeed, one which even the Athenians
themselves did not take to immediately, I wanted to
know what made him choose this play. This is how he
justified it.

It is generally assumed that Greek tragedy is both ele-
mental and unsophisticated, but this is not true. We think
of the actors today leaping about the stage and falling into
prophetic trances, but Greek actors were, in fact, highly
stylized and wore special masks and boots. Classic drama
is essentially as artificial as it is rigorous. It is first and
foremost a liturgy which sets out to impress the audience
rather than to move them. Its horror is majestic, its cru-
elty is solemn. This is true of Aeschylus, who wrote for a
public who still believed in the great myths and in the
mysterious power of the gods. But it is even more true of
Euripides who marks the end of one tradition and the
transition to another, the comedies typified by Menander.
When Euripides wrote *The Trojan Women*, these myths
were already becoming suspect. Although it was too early
to overthrow the old idols, the critical minds of the
Athenians were already questioning them. The play has
its liturgical element. One can see that the Athenians
have already become more interested in what the drama-
tist is saying than how it is said. Though the audience was
offered many of the traditional gestures for which it had
a connoisseur's taste, yet it reacted to these with a new
detachment. From being a mere ritual, tragedy now became a vehicle for thought. Though Euripides used the
traditional form which superficially resembled that of his
predecessors, he knew that his audience was critical of his
content, and consequently his play carries overtones even

when he is writing within the convention. Beckett and Ionesco are doing the same thing today, that is, using a convention to destroy a convention. This method is sound strategy and it also makes for good drama. The Athenians probably reacted to *The Trojan Women* much the same way that contemporary audiences received *Waiting for Godot* or *The Bald-headed Prima Donna*. That is, they were aware that they were listening to characters who had beliefs which they no longer held themselves.

All of which makes a translator's job very difficult. If he keeps to the text he finds himself writing lines like: "*The dawn breaks on white wings*" and producing a romantic pastiche. Though I kept to the classic form, I was not unaware that I was writing for an audience which no longer subscribes to the religious beliefs which the play carries, and therefore would only receive them in inverted commas. Whereas the translation published by Bude, which is excellent in many respects, attempts to reassert those beliefs rather than accept the fact that they are no longer valid. The same problem will arise in four or five centuries from now when Beckett's and Ionesco's comedies are revived. That is, how to bridge the gap which separates the audience from the climate of opinion that obtained when the plays were written.

There was an implicit rapport between Euripides and the audience for which he was writing. It is something which we can see but not share. Since this relationship was implicit, a translation cannot reproduce it. It was therefore necessary to adapt the play.

It would have done no good to try to imitate the style of its language. It would have been equally unprofitable to try to render it into the contemporary French idiom. What I tried to do was to find a style that would be both acceptable to the modern ear and yet sufficiently removed from it to give the play its proper perspective.

I decided to write in verse in order to maintain the liturgical and rhetorical character of the original. I kept the language supple, modified the accent so that my verse could carry the contemporary idiom. As I have said, Euripides wrote for a sophisticated audience which no longer wholly subscribed to the legends he referred to and he was thus able to obtain some ironic effects by reference to them. But my problem was to make the audience take these myths sufficiently seriously to be surprised when they discover that they are no longer effective. We can, of course, still respond to a good deal of Euripides' humour, especially in the character of Talthybios, the prototype of the middleman who is the instrument in events which do not concern him. Our reaction to Helen is, of course, now tainted by Offenbach. Euripides himself could afford to be reckless. He was writing against a solid cultural and religious background, a stability which no longer exists. I therefore had to construct some of this conformity of belief before I could, as it were, destroy it.

The question of style is one thing, but the problems
which arise because of the differences between Greek cul-
ture and our own are altogether another. Euripides' text
contains innumerable allusions which the Athenian public
immediately understood. These mean nothing to us; we
have forgotten the legends to which they refer. Consequently I deleted many of them and developed others.
Cassandra did not have to explain herself to a Greek audience, nor tell them at length what would be Hecuba's
final fate. Everybody knew only too well that, transformed
into a dog, she would climb the mast of the ship which
was to carry her from Troy and then fall into the water.
But when we see her go off at the end of the play, we do
not know this: we believe that she goes to Greece. What
I had to stress was that all Cassandra's predictions came
to pass. Ulysses would take ten years to find his way home,
the Greek navy would be destroyed, Hecuba would never
leave Trojan soil. And to emphasize the tragic dénoue-
ment, I found it necessary to add Poseidon's final mono-
logue.

Similarly the Athenian audience knew only too well
that Menelaus, after having rejected Helen, would end up
by taking her on his own boat. In Euripides the chorus
makes a discreet allusion to this. But there is nothing in
the original text to enable a French audience to anticipate
this sudden change after Menelaus' previous protestation.
It was therefore necessary to make the chorus express the

indignation which the audience feels at this point, when the ship carried Menelaus and Helen away.

In some respects I have modified the general style of the play itself. *The Trojan Women* is not a tragedy in the sense that *Antigone* is: it is more of an oratorio. I have therefore tried to increase the dramatic tensions implicit in the original text by emphasizing some of the conflicts, such as that between Andromeda and Hecuba, the ambivalent attitude of Hecuba herself who, at times, is content to abandon Troy to its misfortune, while at others she rails against the injustice which has caused it. And the sudden switch of that little bourgeoise, Andromeda, who first produces all the attitudes of a wife, and then switches to those of a mother. And finally I emphasized the erotic perversity of Cassandra, who throws herself into Agamemnon's bed, knowing that she will perish there.

These difficulties, you may say, do not justify the choice of the play. But I think its subject does. *The Trojan Women* was produced during the Algerian War, in a very faithful translation by Jacqueline Moatti. I was impressed by the way this version was received. I admit it was the subject of this play which first interested me. That is not surprising. The play had a precise political significance when it was first produced. It was an explicit condemnation of war in general, and of imperial expeditions in particular. We know today that war would trigger off an atomic war in which there would be neither victor nor vanquished.* The play demonstrates this fact precisely: that war is a defeat to humanity. The Greeks destroy Troy but they receive no benefit from their victory. The gods punish their belligerence by making them perish themselves. The message is that men should avoid war. This is Cassandra's affirmation, which is taken so much for granted that it is unnecessary to state it. The effects are obvious enough. It is sufficient to leave the final statement to Poseidon: *Can't you see war will kill you, all of you?*

The only place where I have actually interpolated anything new into the text was in reference to the colonial war where I allowed myself to use the word Europe which is, of course, a wholly modern term. I did so because it is the equivalent of the ancient antagonism which existed between the Greeks and the barbarians, that is, between Greece and the civilization around the Mediterranean, and the gradual infiltration into Asia Minor where colonial imperialism arose. It was this colonialism of Greece into Asia Minor that Euripides denounced, and where I use the expression "dirty war" in reference to these expeditions I was, in fact, taking no liberties with the original text.

I did not tamper with any references to the deities. Their position in the drama is extremely interesting. I have kept close to Euripides here. The only thing I have done is to try to re-state the gods' position, so as to make the criticism of them intelligent to a contemporary audience. In *The Trojan Women* these deities are powerful and ridiculous at the same time. On the one hand they dominate the world. The Trojan War is entirely their work, but we see that they do not conduct themselves as gods but rather as men suffering from human vanities, grudges and jealousies. "*The gods have broad backs,*" Hecuba says when Helen blames them for the consequences of her own bad conduct. In the prologue we see that the goddess betrays her own heavenly colleagues for so little that we are shocked by it. It is as if she had sold heaven for the price of a lipstick. One sees that Euripides' purpose is to use the convention only to destroy it; he accepts a traditional belief only to make it appear ridiculous. The moving prayer which Hecuba makes to Zeus, which so astonishes Menelaus, and seems to anticipate a sort of fervent religiousness à la Renan, suggests that the chaos of human events finally has to submit to divine reason, and appears credible, at least for a moment, for we then see that Zeus has no more respect for human values than either his wife or his daughter. He himself does nothing to save Troy from its fate, and it is one of the paradoxes of the play that the only thing that brings the gods together is their determination to destroy Troy. The play ends in total nihilism. But whereas the Greeks had to live with gods who were capricious, we, seeing their predicament from outside, realize that they were, in fact, rejected by the deities. I have tried to emphasize this, and Hecuba's final despair is the human reply to Poseidon's terrible ultimatum, in which the gods break at last with men and leave them to commune with their own death. This is the final note of tragedy.

JEAN-PAUL SARTRE

(From an article by Bernard Pingaud in *Bref*, the monthly journal of the Théâtre National Populaire, February 1965.)

## A NOTE ABOUT THE
## ENGLISH VERSION

I must stress that this version is a free adaptation and not a translation. A casual comparison between the English and French texts would show that I have taken as many liberties with M. Sartre as he has with Euripides. I have paraphrased some passages and deleted others: cutting many references to the gods and paring Andromeda's dirge. With Racine in the background, the French have still an appetite for rhetoric which a contemporary English-speaking audience will not swallow. I have merely sought to give this version impact and I am sure that M. Sartre, being a man of the theatre, does not object to the liberties I have taken.

RONALD DUNCAN

# THE TROJAN WOMEN

*Characters in order of speaking:*

POSEIDON

PALLAS ATHENE

HECUBA

CHORUS LEADER

CHORUS

TALTHYBIOS

CASSANDRA

ANDROMACHE

ASTYANAX

HELEN

MENELAUS

SOLDIERS

The action takes place by the walls of Troy.
The play is performed without an interval.

~~~~~~~~

# SCENE ONE

[POSEIDON *enters*]

POSEIDON:    I, Poseidon, God of the Sea,
        Have abandoned my shoal of lively Neireides
            And risen from the deep
        To gaze upon this bonfire that was Troy.
            Many years ago with our own hands Phoebus
                and I
        Piled stone upon stone
            And built the walls of that proud city;
                Since then,
        I have loved every stone of it.

[*Pause. He looks down at the ruins*]

        Nothing but ash will be left.
        Now there are no priests in the sacred groves:
            Only corpses.
        Our temples bleed. The Greeks laid waste to
                every one.
        On the very steps of the altar to Zeus,
        King of all the Gods, and my own brother,
            They slit Priam's throat.

[*Pause*]

These Grecian vandals, who sacked my city,
  Will carry their plunder off with them
    To deck out their wives and children
  With the gold and jewels of Phrygia.
Ten times the season for sowing the corn
      came round.
  Still the Greeks stayed there, watching,
    growing old,
Obstinately besieging the city.
    But now it's all over.
Their ships are ready and only wait for the wind.
    It is not courage, but cunning
      which triumphs.
Now the Trojans are dead: all of them,
  But these are their women:
Some to become officers' concubines; others
    mere slaves.
  That one over there with a fat belly,
Is the poor Queen. She is weeping,
  Grieving for her husband and her sons.
It is I who have been defeated;
  For now who will serve or worship me
In all these streets of ash? Nobody.
  Hera, my own sister-in-law, Goddess of
    Argos;

My niece, Pallas Athene, Goddess of Attica,
Combined their powers to destroy my
precious Phrygians:
To break my heart.
I am defeated: I give in.
What can I do with these ruins?
Farewell, noble city,
I shall never look upon your ramparts
Or gaze upon your glistening towers again.
My masterpiece is destroyed. Farewell!
But for Pallas Athene's spite
Proud Troy would stand here still.

## SCENE TWO

[PALLAS enters and goes up to him]

PALLAS: Poseidon!

[He turns, sees her and angrily goes to leave]

No, stay
Most powerful God, whom we lesser

deities worship,
Whom my own Father looks up to.

POSEIDON: When you're polite, Athene, you put me on
my guard.

PALLAS: If I can put our undying hatred to one side
Will you listen to me?

POSEIDON: Why not?
It's always pleasant to have a family chat
Amongst mortal enemies.

PALLAS: Quite. Let's be civilized.
I've a proposition to make.
It's to our mutual interest: it concerns Troy.

POSEIDON: You can see yourself what's left of it.
It's a little late to have any regrets.

PALLAS: Don't worry. I'm not going to feign sorrow
over your city.
I decided to wipe it from the face of the earth.
And that's what I did.

[Pause]

What I want to do is to punish
those Greeks.

POSEIDON:   The Greeks?

PALLAS:   None other. Will you help me?

POSEIDON:   But they're your allies. You've only just given
                them this victory.
                    For the Goddess of Reason, aren't you being
                    a trifle unreasonable?
                I've never known any other God switch so
                    capriciously as you do
                                from love to hate.

PALLAS:   They have insulted me. Cassandra took refuge
                in my temple.
                Ajax dragged her out of it by her hair.
                And do you know not a single Greek
                    Lay a hand on him or tried to prevent him
                        from perpetrating
                This piece of sacrilegious profanity. Not one.
                And to top that, the temple dedicated to me
                    now burns.

POSEIDON:   Mine too.

PALLAS:       Both of us desecrated.
                Will you help me?

[POSEIDON *hesitates*]

And comfort your Trojan dead?

POSEIDON:     You are my niece. But you have done me a
                        terrible injury:
              Don't imagine I shall forget it,
              Or omit to take my revenge.
              But I will help you.

PALLAS:       We must bring about a catastrophic
                        return journey.
                  Zeus has promised me rain, hail and
                        a hurricane
              And will hurl his shafts of lightning against
                        their fragile fleet.
                  You must gather up all your waves
              Into one great wall of water.
                  And when it is as high as a mountain
                  Fling it down upon them.
                  As for those who reach the Straits of Euboea,
              Let the sea open up beneath them
                  To suck them all down to oblivion.
              Let every single one drown;
                        So long as Greece learns respect for me.

POSEIDON:         It shall be done.
                  On the beaches of Mykonos, from Scyros
                        to Lemnos,

> Against the reefs of Delos,
> At the base of the promontory of Caphareus,
> My innumerable mouths shall vomit
> their corpses.
> Return to Olympus, niece. Watch.
> When they start to cast off their ropes
> Ask your father to send down his thunderbolts.

[*They part, each to his side of the stage*]

## SCENE THREE

[HECUBA *is now seen for the first time. She is lying on the ground*]

HECUBA [*Trying to get up*]:

> Up you get, you poor old crone,
> Never mind your broken neck. You're on your
> knees today: but tomorrow you may fall
> on your feet.
> Be patient, philosophical.
> Being sorry for yourself won't get you anywhere;
> It never does, it never did.

Don't try to swim against the current,
    When destiny wants to destroy you: let it.
But it's no use:

                            Not even my courage
Can stand up to the flood of my grief
    In its full spate of sorrow.
Now there is no sorrow in all the world
    Which is not my sorrow.
I was a Queen: my husband, a King.
    I bore him fine sons.
The Greeks cut them down, one by one.

As for my husband, Priam,
These same eyes that weep,
    Watched when they bled him on the steps of
        the altar
And saw his throat open like a mouth
    And his blood flower, then flow, over his
        golden skin;
While my daughters,
    Who were to be betrothed
To the greatest kings of Asia,
They have all been dragged off to Europe
    As chattels to bad masters.

    O Troy,
Your full sails were bellowed with your
            own glory.

They cracked in the sun and sagged.
It was only hot air that had filled them.

[*Pause*]

I talk too much, but I cannot remain silent.
 And silence cannot feel any more than
   words can.
Shall I then weep? I cannot: I have no tears left
   within me.
 I can only throw my body upon the
   indifferent ground
And let it mourn noiselessly
   rolling from side to side
   like an old hulk in a tempest.

[*She goes to throw herself down again, but stops*]

  No.
Misery is like loneliness in this:
 that both are left a voice with which to sing.
That's where all song comes from,
  So I shall sing:

 O ships of Troy,
Did you know where you were going
 ten years ago
When your rowers sweated
And your proud beams parted
 The passive seas of the world?

When every port was your harbour
Did you know then where you were heading?
   All your voyages had one destination;
  You were going to seek that Grecian traitor,
Helen, wife to Menelaus,
    and bring her back to be
    Death to every Trojan.

   O ships of Troy,
From those white decks iron men
    once sprung,
For ten long years now you have lain
Anchored in our own harbours.
But today you are to sail away again
Taking me, the Queen of your city, with you
   With shaven head and ravaged face

To be a servant at a servant's table.
Did you have to do all this for this:
   To bring a blood bath on my people,
Plunge me and all these women
    into mourning,
All because you wanted the glory once again
   Of sailing across to Greece
   To anchor where shame is fathomless?

[*She claps her hands*]

   Get up there

> You Trojan widows, Trojan virgins, all mated
> to the dead.
> Have the guts to look down upon these
> smouldering ruins
> For the last time
> And articulate your grief.

LEADER OF THE CHORUS:
> Your anguish, Hecuba, has ripped
> open our tent.
> Fear feeds at our breasts,
> Claws at our hearts.
> What do you want us to do?

HECUBA: Look down at those ships in the bay.

A WOMAN: The Greeks are hoisting their sails.

ANOTHER WOMAN: I can see men carrying oars.

ALL: They are leaving.

LEADER [To others off-stage]:
> Come out and see what's in store for you.
> The Greeks are getting ready to go home,
> You poor wretches, come out here and see
> for yourselves.
> All of you!

HECUBA:     No, no, not all of you.
            Not Cassandra. Keep her inside. She's mad.
            At least spare me the last humiliation
               Of letting the Greeks see me blush
                  with shame.

A WOMAN:    What will they do?
            Put us to the sword?

ANOTHER WOMAN:   Abduct us, ravage us?

HECUBA:     Think of the worst.
               It will be that.

   [*To herself*]

                  A slave.
               Whose? Where?
                  In Argos? in Phthia?
            On some island off the coast?
                  A pitiful old woman
                  More dead than alive,
               A useless hornet in a foreign hive,
                  Dragging out her last few days.
            Or I will have to squat night and day
                  Outside somebody's door
                     at their beck and call;
                  As nurse to some Greek matron's brats;

> Or worse, stuck in their kitchen baking
>> bitter bread;
> With nothing but rags to cover the ruins of
>> my body
> And only an earth floor to lie down upon.

[Pause]

> And I was Queen of Troy.

A WOMAN:    If I throw my shuttle from side to side for ever
            It will never be on the looms of Ida again.

ANOTHER WOMAN:   Every member of my family is dead.
                My home burned to the ground.
                Looking on these walls which smell so acrid
            I know that I am seeing them for the last time.

LEADER:     Be quiet.
            Preserve your strength,
            Worse misfortunes yet await you.

A WOMAN:    Are there worse than these?

ANOTHER WOMAN:   Yes. One night some drunken Greek
                Will drag you to his filthy bed.

FIRST WOMAN:    The thought of what my body may do
                Makes me loath each limb of it.

OTHER WOMAN:   Uprooted.
　　　　To live away from here will be to live in hell.

ANOTHER WOMAN:   I shall probably have to carry
　　　　their slops.

ANOTHER WOMAN:   Maybe I'll be a servant in Attica?
　　　　On the fertile plain of Penee,
　　At the foot of Mount Olympus.
　　　　They say life is good there,
　　　　Even for slaves.

FIRST WOMAN:   Anything's better than to be taken to the
　　　　banks of the Eurotas.
　　　There I'd see Helen triumphant
　　　And have to obey Menelaus,
　　　The butcher of Troy.

LEADER:   Someone's coming.

OTHERS:   Who is it?

LEADER:   A Greek. Look how he runs.
　　　　He's coming to tell us what they're going to
　　　　do with us.
　　　This is the end. Though we haven't yet left our
　　　native land,

We are foreign to it;
  As we are now things that belong to Greece,
Their slaves. Even here, their slaves.


## SCENE FOUR


[Enter TALTHYBIOS. *He speaks to* HECUBA]

TALTHYBIOS: You know who I am, noble lady,
   Talthybios, herald to the Greek Army.
  I often entered the gates of your city,
   To deliver messages from our generals.
  And I am now instructed to convey an edict
   to you.

HECUBA:  The moment we feared has come.

TALTH: I suppose it has: your future has been decided.

HECUBA:  Where are we to go?

TALTH: You are all to be separated.
  Each to different masters.

HECUBA:     What masters?
            Are we all to be treated exactly alike?
            No exception made for anyone?
            Surely not?

TALTH:   No. Give me time: I will tell you

HECUBA:   I am waiting.

[Pause]

            Cassandra?

TALTH:      You've guessed right.
            She is to be one of the lucky ones:
            Agamemnon himself wants your daughter.

HECUBA:     As a servant to Clytemnestra?
            It is as I feared.

TALTH:      Not at all.
            The King of Kings wants her as his concubine.

HECUBA:     His harlot?

TALTH:   He might even marry her . . . in secret.

HECUBA:   So.

You know that she is already betrothed to
the Sun,
To him alone,
And that the golden-headed god
insists she remain a virgin.

TALTH: Of course. It's because her virginity can be
guaranteed, she being a prophetess,
That she's so attractive to His Majesty.

HECUBA: Throw away the temple keys, poor child;
Tear off your holy fillet
And cover your hair with ash.

TALTH: Come now, worse things could happen to her
Than sharing a bed with a King.

HECUBA: And what have you done with my
daughter Polyxena?

TALTH: She serves Achilles.

HECUBA: But Achilles is dead.

TALTH: She still serves him.

HECUBA: What strange customs you Greeks have.

To think that I gave her life
For her to spend it in a tomb.

TALTH: She's one of the lucky ones, I can tell you.
Even Cassandra will often wish she was
with her.

HECUBA: Why?

TALTH: She has found peace there.

HECUBA: Is she alive? Can she still see the sky
Or the stars at night?
Tell me.
Your look of shame's your answer.

TALTH: We have given her shelter.

HECUBA: Shelter from what?

TALTH: The world.

HECUBA: True.

[Pause]

And Andromeda?

TALTH: Well, of course, being Hector's wife,
She was considered something special
And goes to Achilles' son.

HECUBA:   And what of me? Broken with age,
            Unable to walk without this stick.
            What work can I do?
            Who could possibly want me?

TALTH:   Ulysses. A slave in his household.

HECUBA:     No. No. Anybody but him.
            I spit on that dog.
          On that double-tongued monster
            Who breathes hatred and discord
          Wherever he finds friendship.
          Ulysses! O Women of Troy,
          Now weep for me, your Queen
            in Misery alone.

CHORUS:   And what about us?
          What is to become of us?

TALTH:   How should I know?
          It's not my business.
          The small fry will be sorted out in lots.
    [To the GUARDS]

            Go and fetch Cassandra.
              Agamemnon wants her within the hour.
            What's that? The tent's all red.
              Quick, stop any Trojan women
            From burning themselves alive.

>    I can understand that a free people
>    Don't easily knuckle under to a catastrophe
>       like this,
>    But I don't want any embarrassing suicides on
>       my hands.
>    Do you understand?
>    And certainly no human torches.
>    That might be a way out for them
>    But it would be a bore to me.

HECUBA:   No fire there at all.
          It's Cassandra.
          She's gone mad.


## SCENE FIVE

[*Enter* CASSANDRA]

CASSANDRA:   May this flame,
             This gentle flame,
                Rise slowly, dance fiercely,
             Round this torch of me,

And lift its impetuous pride
  Against the thighs of night
And stand up straight within the supple air.
  May Hymen bless the union that it makes
And grant that I, who was a virgin of the sun,
  Shall its full quietus make, as I lie beside
    the King.

[*To* HECUBA]

  Hold this torch, Mother,
  Lead the cortege.
What's wrong? Why are you crying?
  Because of my father, because of my brothers?
It is too late to grieve for them
    For I am to be married,
    Your tears should be of joy, of joy!
      Take it.

[*She holds out the torch to* HECUBA]

  You refuse? Very well,
    My own hands shall coax and carry this flame
    To Hymen's couch
  Where a Greek is to take me.
For even if the Queen of the Night
Set alight to all her stars,
    And the entrails of the hemisphere debowled
      burned in their orbits

I would not have light enough:
Darkness would mark my way
    As I walked toward that bed
        Where I am to be joined to the enemy.

So may this flame rise higher and higher
            till it licks the sky,
For this is the day my life has grown to.
        Now Phoebus, God that is my God,
        Conduct this choir that is my choir,
    And you, my Mother, dance;
    Join in this dance for her who was
            your daughter.
Oh please, Mother, to please me . . .
    And why are these Women of Troy
Not dressed for a carnival and
        singing hilariously?
Come, now all together, after me:
    Oh woe, woe, woe.


LEADER OF THE CHORUS:

    [TO HECUBA]

        Hold her back, Your Majesty,
    Hold on to her,
            She doesn't know what she's doing
            And might even jump straight into his bed.

HECUBA: Give me that torch, child,
　　　　You're not holding it upright.

CHORUS: Her ecstasy is all despair,
　　　　　Misery has not made her sane.

CASSANDRA: They think that I'm mad.
　　　　　　Listen, Mother, I tell you
　　　You should rejoice at this betrothal.
　　　　　And if you see me
　　　　　suddenly timid,
　　　I want you to thrust me into Agamemnon's
　　　　　arms and let him carry me off to Argos.
　　For once there, I will turn our marriage bed
　　　　into his tomb.
　　Helen had a thousand thousand Greeks killed
　　　　beneath our walls.
　　But I shall do even worse to them.
　　　　Cassandra will be their doom.
　　Through me, and because of me,
　　　　Their King, their great King, shall perish.
　　By my sacrifice their royal house shall fall.
　　And I shall destroy his people
　　　　As he has destroyed our own.
　　So now is not the time to weep
　　Unless tears of joy,
　　　　So laugh as the wind laughs;

Let there be a gale of laughter;
For I swear my father and my brothers
will be revenged.

HECUBA:     How? By you?

CASSANDRA:   By me.

HECUBA:     My child, you will be a slave, helpless . . .
How can you . . . ?

CASSANDRA:   With an axe.
There, right in the skull.
I'm not saying it will be I who strikes the blow,
But I guarantee this King of Kings will bleed
all the same.
Oh, how he'll bleed!

[Joyfully]

As for me, they'll cut my throat.

[Pause]

A long time later, the son will kill his
own Mother
And flee—dogs at his heels.
That will be the end of the House of Atreus.
Nobody will ever fear them again.

CHORUS:     Don't, Cassandra.
            You are embarrassing us,
        And you are making your Mother feel ashamed.
            Not in front of the Greeks, we beg you . . .
                Don't let our conquerors
                Hear your prophecies
                And smile at your distraction.


CASSANDRA:   Why should I be silent?
            I speak only of what the Sun has told me.
                I could tell you more
                    But it is too horrible.
                You are right. I will say no more.

[To HECUBA]

                Don't cry.
            The Greeks are victorious. But what now?
                What happens to them?
            I will tell you:
                they will be beaten, they will be humiliated:
            Some will fall outside Troy, others on the plains.
                They will perish in their thousands,
            Not in defence of a city on their native land
                As our men did:
                They will die for nothing.
            Few of them will ever see their homes again,
                They will not even be buried;

Nobody will say a prayer over them;
Trojan earth will digest their flesh
And their wives will never find their bones.
These wretches are all recruits,
a slaughtered but unburied army.
The vultures wait,
And oblivion awaits them.
Not a trace of these conquerors will remain;
Not even their shadow.
Except for a handful
who will crawl back to Greece
Only to find themselves unwanted
and unwelcome.
Apollo himself has told me
How Clytemnestra has behaved in
Agamemnon's absence.
But I won't repeat it.
And all this, for what?
Ten years to seek out one adulteress;
And their victory will be to find
Their own wives have been faithless
to them—
And every man's a cuckold!

[To TALTHYBIOS]

This is what you call winning the war.
True, we have lost it;

But not our honour.
We have fallen on our own soil
Defending our own city.
Gentle hands waited to nurse our wounds,
And watching eyes waited to weep
When we could bleed no more.
When our King fell
Troy itself was his widow.

[*To* HECUBA]

You should be grateful to these Greeks.
They even turned Hector
Who was a modest gentle man
Into an immortal legend of courage.
We who defended our native land
are glorified,
But those who conquered us shall be cursed.
They started this filthy war:
They will die as stupidly as they lived.

[*To the* TROJAN WOMEN]

Lift up your heads: be proud,
Leave your revenge to me;
He who embraces me will be destroyed by me.

A WOMAN:   I wish I could believe you;
I wish I could laugh

And be as crazily defiant as you are.
　　But look at us,
　Take a look at yourself.
All your singing and spitting won't get
　　　　you anywhere.
　It's all words,
　　　impotent words.

TALTHYBIOS:　　And they'd prove rather expensive
　　　　If we didn't know she was insane.

[Aside]

The more I see of the intimate lives of the great
　　The more I realize they're as petty and
　　　　　perverse as the next man.
　As for the most mighty King of Argos
Who has taken it into his head
　　to desire this creature who's not right in hers,
All I can say is: a poor devil like me
　　Wouldn't want her for all the gold in all
　　　　　the world.
　　But there it is:
So come on, my pretty, follow us.
　　Let's get going.
　　You heard them: words won't help you now.

[To HECUBA]

I'll come back for you

Immediately Ulysses sends for you.
    You won't find it so bad with him,
As servant to Penelope.
    People speak rather well of her.

CASSANDRA:    Servant? There's only one servant here
            And that: you,
        You insolent and obsequious lout
    With the manners of a farm hand.
        You don't know what you're talking about.
    My Mother won't be going to Ithaca.
        Apollo has assured me
            She will die here, in Troy.

TALTH:    Not if I have anything to do with it, she won't.
        Her suicide would finish me.

CASSANDRA:    Who said anything about suicide?

TALTH:        How else?

CASSANDRA:    You'd like to know, wouldn't you?
            But I shan't tell you.
        As for Ulysses and all his double talk,
            That man doesn't know what he's in for.
            He's got another ten years,
        Another ten years of mud and blood,
            before he sees Ithaca again.

Oh yes, I know everything's ready and he's
about to set sail,
But the end is often only another beginning.
The giant flesh-eating Cyclops
squats on his rock,
his mouth watering, waiting for him.
So does Circe who turns men into pigs;
Not to mention Scylla and Charybdis
who lick their lips at a smell of a shipwreck.
I tell you the only place Ulysses is going to
is Hell.
We know a few who are waiting for
him there.

[*To the* WOMEN]

I can assure you Ulysses will suffer.
Whatever your misfortunes are,
He will envy them.

[*She looks into the distance*]

That's it. When he eventually climbs out
of Hades
And lands on his own island
He finds that it too has been conquered.

[*She emerges from her trance*]

But what's Ulysses to me?

[*To* talthybios]

> Well, what are we waiting for?
> I'm impatient to be joined to my betrothed:
>> for better or worse.
>> No, just the worst.
>> So toll the wedding bells!
> Our marriage shall be a cortege down the road
>> to Hell
> And this generalissimo,
>> this King of Kings,
> Who wants to embrace the daughter of the Sun
>> Will never see the light again.
> Endless night will devour you,
>> And your body will be chucked over a cliff.
>> Toll the wedding bells!
> For our broken bodies will be naked together
>> And vultures alone will be satisfied;
> Their beaks will be intimate with my breast;
>> Their claws shall caress your manhood.
> Here I'll tear the veil of my virginity,
>> Of prophecy,
> While my body is still unravished.
> May the gentle breeze
>> waft it to the true God of Love:
>> The Sun, the Sun.
>> Now which is my boat? Where do I embark?
> Since I am death,

See that a black flag
    Flies at the mast of the ship which carries me.
Goodbye, Mother,
    Be calm; you're going to die soon.
Father, I am coming,
    I am coming to join you in your grave;
I won't keep you waiting,
    I am coming to you at the head of a
        hideous cortege
        Made up of the entire House of Atrides
        Who slaughtered you.
        Toll the wedding bells!

[*She goes off with the* SOLDIERS]

Dong! Dong!
Toll the wedding bells!

[HECUBA *faints*]

LEADER OF THE CHORUS:    Quick, Hecuba's collapsed.
        Don't stand there. Lift her gently:
        She's still our Queen.

[*They do so*]

HECUBA:    I did not seek your concern
        And I do not thank you for it.
        What I wanted was to embrace the earth,
            to yield myself into its blind unconsciousness.

For you see, we are all blind too;
　　We can do nothing but submit.
But unhappily, though we are blind,
　　we alone are conscious.

CHORUS:　　Oh Royal Lady,
　　　　Pray to the Gods.

HECUBA [*Savagely*]:
　　　　No. They are allies
　　Not to be relied upon.
　　　　Let us be silent.

CHORUS:　　　Silence is something we fear.

HECUBA:　　Then stop complaining.
　　Better, think when you were last happy.

CHORUS [*Alternating verses*]:
　　　　That was yesterday.
　　It was only yesterday
　　　　that we were happy.
　　That was the same day Troy fell.
　　　　In the morning, we saw from the ramparts
　　That the beach was deserted
　　　　And their fleet had left our bay;
　　There in the middle of the plain
　　　　Stood a great wooden horse on wheels,

A wooden horse with a golden harness.
The people of Troy, seeing this idol
From the rock of the citadel,
cried out: "It is over. The siege is finished.
The Greeks are gone. Our suffering is at an end,
So hoist their wooden idol into our Acropolis
As an offering to Pallas Athene,
Zeus' noble daughter, who has forgiven us."
Everyone was shouting and singing;
Strangers kissed in the streets;
Old men asked what all the excitement
was about.
"It's peace, it's peace," we cried,
and lifted them off their feet.
We tethered ropes round this idol to haul it to
Athene's Temple.
Everyone lent a hand, some pulling,
others pushing.
It took all day, not till dusk was it there;
Then our victory songs and the sound of Lydian
lutes enlivened the night.
That was yesterday.
All the houses in the city were dark
and empty;
Everybody was out in the streets: dancing
with torches,
Singing; nobody slept, it was a night of carnival,

A carnival of peace.
　　That was how Troy went down:
In riotous joy!
　　And that was only yesterday.

**LEADER OF THE CHORUS:**
　　Nothing is more deceptive than happiness.
　　Joy is a cheat which covers up for the misery
　　　　stalking behind the grin.
　　At midnight we were still singing,
　　　　then suddenly the whole city
　　　　rang with one refrain:
　　　　　　it was the cry
　　　　　　　　of death.
　　　　War was back again:
　　　　Pallas had forgiven nothing.
　　The Greeks had leapt out of the idol
　　And were slaughtering our men and boys.
　　　　That was how our night of celebration ended
　　　　　　with the dawn of death.

**HECUBA:**　　Troy wasn't conquered:
The Trojans weren't defeated.
　　They were betrayed by a Goddess:
It's always a mistake to worship a woman.

**LEADER OF THE CHORUS:**　　Look, Your Majesty,
　　　　　　A chariot is coming.

[HECUBA *doesn't move*]

A WOMAN:   It's Andromeda, Hector's wife,
                    carrying Astyanax in her arms.

[*To* ANDROMEDA]

          Where are you taking him?

ANDROMEDA:   To my master.

[HECUBA *now turns, looks coldly at* ANDROMEDA, *and sees* ASTYANAX *who carries a small basket*]

HECUBA:   Misery. Everywhere I look: misery.

ANDROMEDA:   What are you crying about?
                        It's my loss.

HECUBA:   It's ours.

ANDROMEDA: No, mine.

HECUBA:   You are all my children.

ANDROMEDA: Were.

HECUBA:   I mourn for all my sons.

ANDROMEDA: But I only for one, Hector.

HECUBA:      I weep for our burning city.

ANDROMEDA: I weep for Hector's city.

HECUBA:      For our royal home.

ANDROMEDA: Only for the house where I became
                    a woman:
                  Where I gave birth to Astyanax.

HECUBA:      It's burning: it's burnt.
                  Everything's flattened: a shambles of ash.

ANDROMEDA:   You are to blame.
                  It was you who gave birth to Paris:
                       that damned adventurer.
                  Didn't the Gods themselves, foreseeing
                       his future,
                     order you to smother him?
                  You refused: it is we who are punished for that:
                       for your pride
                     Which you hawked around as a
                          Mother's love.
                  It was this precious infant of yours
                     Which smashed Troy like a toy;
                     And now Pallas alone can laugh
                  At the heap of corpses piled up at the foot of
                          her statue,

While these vultures encircle us;
and we stand here as slaves.

HECUBA [*Broken, her face in her hands*]:
> If Priam
> could cry out from Hell
> He would shout: "You lie, you lie."

ANDROMEDA:   If Hector could come back
> He would save me. He would revenge me.

[*Then quietly but without gentleness*]

> I have never liked you.
> You have never liked me.
> But you're an old woman:
> I feel sorry for you.

[*Pause*]

> Polyxena is dead.

HECUBA:   Dead? What a coward I am.
> That's what Talthybios was trying to tell me.
> And I hadn't the courage to understand.
> Dead. How?

ANDROMEDA:   They cut her throat on Achilles' tomb.

[*Pause*]

I saw her body.
I covered her face with a black veil.

HECUBA:   Slaughtered on a tomb:
Like a goat, or an ox.
    What a terrible death.

ANDROMEDA:   Why terrible?
She is dead. That's all.
    Better off than I who live.

HECUBA:   What do you know of death or life?
I tell you death is a nothingness;
    however painful life is
        it is better than death: it has hope.
I prefer life at its worst to death at its best.

ANDROMEDA:   Your will to live's insane.
    You know very well you've nothing to live for,
        Your sons are all dead,
    And your belly is too old to breed any more.
        Your future is completely hopeless.
            So much the better for you.
    You can give in and sink in your circumstances
        Rather than clinging on to a life
            that's finished
        As far as you're concerned.

If you do that you won't suffer so much.
    For death is a void,
    A void that is eternal and peaceful.
Listen to me: It is the same for Polyxena now
    As it was before she was born.
    For now she is dead, she can't suffer any more,
    and is unaware of the suffering she once
        experienced:
      her sheet is wiped clean again.
But I still suffer, and I still know I suffer:
    Life has more to scribble over me.
I was a good wife and devoted Mother;
    Some of us are. But as many of us know:
It doesn't matter how a woman behaves.
    The world thinks the worst of us,
And slanders us if we give it half a chance.
    I didn't give it that chance. I stayed
      at home,
    Where the gossips couldn't get at me.
It was no sacrifice: I was happy
    Devoting myself wholly to Hector.
But you see, old woman, my virtuous life
    has been my undoing,
And my reputation for being chaste recoils
    on me; for it is that
Which now makes Neoptolemus,
    the son of the man who murdered

my husband,
Demand me for his bed.
I am frightened. I am frightened
And it is myself I fear.
For I do not want my memory of Hector
to be erased.
But I am a woman,
And a woman is only a woman.
They say it takes just one night of pleasure
to master her:
A woman is only an animal.
That is why I am frightened.
Hector was the only man I ever knew;
I loved his courage, his wisdom, and
his gentleness,
The touch of his hands on my body.
And now the thought that this same body
May groan for joy when some other man lies
upon it,
Makes me want to tear it limb from limb.
Polyxena was lucky:
She was murdered still a virgin.

[*To* HECUBA]

Liar. You say life is hope.
Look at me. I'm alive. What hope have I?
None.

I know what life's going to write on me.

LEADER OF THE CHORUS:   You are a Princess,
                    But misfortune levels us.
            By telling us of your fears
                    You make me aware of my own.

HECUBA:   When the sea is rough
            Sailors sail into it bravely;
                    But when there's a tempest,
            They haul their canvasses down,
                    And let the waves drive them where they will.
                        I do that: I yield and I advise you to do
                            the same:
            My child, Hector, is dead. Your tears won't
                        bring him back.
                    Forget him: devote the virtues which he loved
                        to your new husband.

ANDROMEDA:   You disgusting old slut,
                    To think that Hector's own Mother
                    Should turn pimp.
            You're nothing but a whoremonger.

HECUBA:       Do what I say,
                    For Astyanax's sake.
                He is the son of my son,

And the last of his race.
Do it for his sake,
  So that he,
Or his son's son,
May one day refound this city,
  And avenge us.

[*Enter* TALTHYBIOS]

What now?

TALTHYBIOS [*Going to* ANDROMEDA]:
Don't hate me.

ANDROMEDA:   Why not?

TALTHYBIOS:   I am only a messenger.
It is my distasteful duty
  To tell you what my masters have decided.

ANDROMEDA:   Come to the point.
Don't be afraid to speak.

TALTH:   Your son.

ANDROMEDA:   Are they going to separate us?

TALTH:   In a way. Yes.

ANDROMEDA: We shan't have the same masters?

TALTH: He won't have one at all.

ANDROMEDA: You're leaving him here?

TALTH: I don't know how to tell you.

ANDROMEDA: Spare me your scruples,
Get on with your job, lackey.

TALTH: They're going to kill him.

[Pause. She clasps her child to her, staring at him. He continues quickly]

It was Ulysses who persuaded them.
He urged the Greek Assembly
Not to spare the life of the heir to the
Trojan throne,
because he might sometime become the focal
point of rebellion.
The Assembly accepted his resolution.

[Pause]

So it's no use holding on to him like that.
Give him to me.

[She resists]

Come on now. Hand him over.

There's nothing else you can do.
Neither your city, nor your husband,
    can protect you now:
        neither exist any more.
Don't you understand, we give the orders now?
    Do I have to tear him from you?
Don't be silly. Bow to the inevitable,
    Accept it with dignity.

[Pause]

For God's sake, isn't there anything
        that can make you hand that child over?
Can't you see you won't gain anything
        By trying my patience
    Or making the soldiers angry?
If you do that, they'll just leave him to
        the vultures.
But if you hand over quietly,
    we might even let you bury him,
and our generals will treat you with
        more consideration.

ANDROMEDA [*To the* SOLDIERS]:
    Don't you dare lay hands on him!
    I'll hand him over. Later.

[*They back away, watching her. She looks down at her child in silence. Then slowly lifts up its hands one at*

a time, examining the small fingers. She then holds one
of its feet in her hands; then runs her forefinger over
the line of the child's mouth and eyes as though she
had never seen the child, or any child, before. The
SOLDIERS approach her. She looks up. They stop. She
walks towards them holding out the child]

ANDROMEDA:   Here you are, take it: kill it.
Hit it with an axe. Throw it on a fire:
It's yours.
I can't protect it: I could only give life to it.
What are you waiting for?
Take it.

[The SOLDIER goes to lead the child off when ASTYANAX
spills his basket of sea shells. The SOLDIER bends down
to pick them up and places them in the basket, then
leads the child off]

TALTH [To the SOLDIERS]:

Carry it to the ramparts. Wait for me there.

[To himself]

All very distasteful. I feel quite sick.
That's the worst of war:
Those who give the orders
Seldom see the mess it makes
When you hold a child by the feet
And bash its head in against a wall.

HECUBA:    That child was my son's son.
           There goes our future, mine and yours.

[*She puts her hands over her eyes*]

           What a blessing blindness would be.

[*Exeunt* OMNES *except* HECUBA *and* THE CHORUS *It is now
dawn*]

CHORUS:    Once again
           The gentle dawn illumines a burned-out city.
             This is the second time in our history
           The brazen dawn has revealed
             a tangle of limbs in our gutters,
           Rubble spewing over our streets.
             This is the second time
           The Greeks have liberated us.
             The first time, it was many years ago.
           They invaded us from Salamis.
             They told us then that they were bringing
           Greek culture and European enlightenment
             to the backward people of Asia:
             Our city burned with progress,
           Our young men had their limbs
             amputated by philosophy.
           The Greeks always envied our harvests,
             their soil was eroded, ours still fertile;
           That was all there was to it, many years ago.

But that time, though they sacked our city,
    they did not lay waste to the countryside;
They went away
    leaving us with the strength to rebuild.
Our Gods were merciful then.
    But now they have abandoned us.
Though we lift our hands to heaven and cry:
    Save us! Save us!

[A pause]

Nobody answers. Only Echo.
    This dawn is indifferent: our Gods are deaf.

[They sink to the ground. Enter MENELAUS with SOL-
DIERS]

MENELAUS:    What a glorious morning!
    This is the day of all days.
The day I've lived for;
    There that slut sits now
Squatting in a hovel, a prisoner
    at my mercy; I have no mercy.
Now is the moment I have lived for:
    when I caught up with her again,
And could make her suffer
    as she made me suffer . . .
You will have guessed that I'm King Menelaus,
    well known for his misfortunes.

Some people at home criticise me:
  They say I started this terrible war
Merely because of a woman.
  But that's not fair.
It was because of a man.
  And that man was Paris,
The shit whom I took into my palace
  and who ran off with my wife.
That's why this war's been fought.
  And I'm grateful that the Gods
have punished Paris for his perfidy:
  Neither he, nor his city, exist any more.
And now it's this woman's turn:
  this woman whose name sticks in my throat;
Whose name I've never spoken for years,
        ten years.
  I have two alternatives:
Either to have her executed here
  Amongst the ruins of the city she chose
        for her home,
Or to take her back to Sparta
  and settle her account there.
I've decided to do precisely that:
  for by postponing her punishment, I
        increase it.
When she reaches Sparta
  The mothers and widows of the Greeks

Whose men fell here
>> will lynch her, stone her to death;
That'll be her end.

[*To the* SOLDIERS]

>> Get her.
Drag her out by her hair.
>> Make her grovel at my feet.
Then I promise you we'll hoist sails
>> and only wait for a wind.

HECUBA:   At last.

[*Pause*]

>> At last I can believe in you, Zeus.
>>> You,
>>>> the unknown
>>> and the unknowable,
>>>> You,
>> Who seated at the centre of the earth
>>> can, at the same time,
>> hold the world in your hands
>>> like a ball in space,
>>>> at last you have my grudging belief.
>> At any rate, I believe in your justice
>> For by this, I see that you do punish the wicked.

MENELAUS:   That's a strange sort of prayer.
>> Who are you?

HECUBA:   Hecuba, Queen of Troy.

MENELAUS:   I didn't recognize you.

HECUBA:   Are you really going to punish Helen?

MENELAUS:   I gather from your prayer
                that you'd like to see her put to death?

HECUBA:   Of course.

MENELAUS:   So would I. So would I.

HECUBA:   That's what I meant by saying Zeus was just.
                Do it. But when you do it,
                    Don't look at her.

MENELAUS:   Why not? It's ten years since I saw her.
                I want to see what those years
                    have done to her too.

HECUBA:       Nothing. You should know that.
            Women like her keep their beauty
                because life doesn't touch them.
            They're indifferent to the misery they cause.
                They age late and then suddenly.
            Her eyes are still beautiful,
                though death looks out of them;

Her skin is still smooth,
For her lips, men will still slaughter
each other,
and cities burn.

[HELEN *comes out from the tent*]

Go now. Don't look at her.
You think your desire for her is dead.
She will rekindle it,
And you'll be in her clutches again.

MENELAUS: Nonsense.

[*He turns and looks at* HELEN]

[*Pause*]

Release her.

HELEN: You need not have used force
to have me brought to you.
The instant I saw you, I wanted to run to you.
For though you hate me, I still love you.
I have wanted you. I have waited for you.

[*Pause*]

Let me ask you one question:
I will never ask another:
What do you want to do to me?

MENELAUS: I?

HELEN:     You.

MENELAUS:   To kill you.

HELEN:   If you, my love, want my death,
                then I, my love,
                        desire my own death too.
            But just let me explain.

MENELAUS:   No. I don't want to hear your explanations.
                You're going to die. That's all.

HELEN:   Are you afraid to listen?

MENELAUS:   Aren't you afraid to die?

HECUBA:   It's too late now. I begged you not to look.
                But you may just as well let her talk.
                    There's no risk there
                    Whatever she has to say. I have an answer
                        to it.
            And will stuff her lies down her throat,
                So let her talk of your past;
            It will give you the courage
                to see that she has no future.

MENELAUS:   You needn't worry. There's nothing she
                can say
            that will have any effect on me.

But I'll let her talk, since you want me to.
   She knows only too well
There's nothing she can say, or do,
   that will have any effect on me.
She's already dead as far as I'm concerned.


HELEN [*Placing herself in front of him*]:
   No, do not turn away.
     Look at me.
   Have the courage to look at me for the last time.
   Look on every part, then know what it is
     you're killing.
   You hate me? I do not hate you.
     If only you knew . . . Yes,
    There are some things you should know . . .
   Oh, I know the sort of things I've been
     accused of . . .
    But I've an explanation for each.
   I don't know whether you'll believe me or not,
    But let me speak and have the courage
     to listen.

[*Pause*]

   Do you want to know who is really to blame
    for all this misery?
   She is. That old woman. She was the start of
    it all.

It was she who gave birth to Paris.
The Gods themselves were alarmed.
They foresaw that that scoundrel would ferment
   a war—and what a war.
  They ordered her to smother him.
  Did she do it?
No. And King Priam was too weak to make her.
  All of this stems from that;
  That was the beginning of it all.
Paris was only twenty when three Goddesses
  competed for his favours.
Pallas herself offered him the whole of Greece
  if he'd choose her.
And with her behind him
  he'd have overrun it in no time.
And what was Hera's bribe?
  She offered him Asia Minor.
And the whole of Europe.
  But Cypris offered nothing.
Nothing except me. She merely described me.
  She won. Paris chose her for his Goddess,
Then worshipped me.
   You were lucky then.
For if he'd chosen either of the other two,
  he would have conquered Greece.
If it were not for this body,
  which your soldiers have so misused,

You yourself would be a subject of
that barbarian.
But your luck was my misfortune.
That you might escape
I became the victim: Cypris sacrificed me.
And my beauty, my beauty became my shame.

MENELAUS:   You slut. Why did you go?

HELEN:   Darling, it was you, not I, who left.
You were a careless husband
When you went off to Crete
and left me alone with your lecherous guest.

MENELAUS:   You could have resisted.

HELEN:   I, a mere mortal,
Resist the Goddess, Aphrodite?
Could you do that?
A pity you cannot punish her
for what she did to me.
If you could, you'd be stronger than
Zeus himself,
For even the King of the Gods
Is as much her slave as everybody else is.
Why did I go?
That's a question I've often asked myself.

And the answer is always the same:
   It was not I who left,
   But somebody who was not me.
Aphrodite was an unseen guest in your palace,
   like an invisible shadow to Paris;
And as you know, Cypris had made a bargain
         with Paris
   to give me to him as long as he lived.
There was nothing I could do
   to break that odious but sacred tie.
But the moment Paris was dead, I was free.
   Immediately I did everything, everything
         I could
To get back to you.
   At night, I climbed up on the city walls,
Tied ropes together to carry me to the ground
   where I might run to you.
Your own guards can prove it:
   because they always caught me.
That's all I have to say: that's my story.
   I am the victim of circumstance;
Destiny's plaything: abducted;
   married against my will to a man I loathed;
   forced to live in a foreign city I despised.
All this I endured to save my country.
   My own chastity was my contribution;
And there is nothing more precious to a
         woman than that.

Yet, in spite of this sacrifice,
　　they are wanting to stone me to death.
I am hated by the Greeks, detested by
　　　　the Trojans,
Alone in the world, understood by none.
　 Now tell me this:
Do you think it is right to put me to death
When it was the Gods, not I, who sinned?
　 If you don't, then take me where I belong:
In our bed, on your throne;
　 To do less would be to insult the Gods
Who, for all their mistakes,
　　　　do not err in justice.

HECUBA:　　I'm beginning to doubt it.

CHORUS:　　Don't let her get away with it, Your Majesty.
　　　　This woman is dangerous.
　　　　Puncture her eloquence with a few facts.

HECUBA:　　　 Very ingenuous.
　　You'd like us to believe that the three Goddesses
　　　　were as vain as you are?
　　That they would trade their holy cities
　　　　to corrupt a jury at a beauty contest?
　　Is it likely that Hera would give
　　　　Argos sanctuary?

Or Athene would ever deliver Athens to
    the Trojans?
  They were merely teasing Paris.
By trying to suggest that the Goddesses are
    vain too
  You do not diminish your own viciousness.
    As for all this about Aphrodite:
You make me laugh, if I could laugh.
  Though I must say I liked your bit about
    Aphrodite
Entering the palace as a shadow to my son.
  Tell me why would she bother to do that
When she can control us like marionettes
  from the comfort and security of heaven?
If King Menelaus wants to know the truth,
  all he has to do is to remember
  how handsome my son Paris was.
Immediately this woman saw him, she
    wanted him.
  That's all there was to it.
I'm tired of hearing people
  blaming Aphrodite for lusts which are all
    their own.
Paris was very good looking. He stayed with you.
  He was a Prince of Asia:
She was also impressed by the golden ornaments
    he wore.

Greed added to her lust,
She didn't rest till she'd satisfied both desires.

[To HELEN]

You always had to make do with the second
best didn't you?
Sparta is a poor country. There, even the
Queen has
to be economical.
And you wanted luxury:
You wanted to be able to copulate all night
and chuck bucketfuls of gold out of
your windows
during the day.
So you ditched your husband for a man
you lusted
after and traded your shabby little kingdom in
for the richest city in the whole of Asia.
It was good business, wasn't it?
Yet you try to make out you were carried off
against your will.
Will. Odd that nobody saw this abduction.
Strange you didn't cry out.
Or if you did nobody heard you.
And when your own people declared war,
Came here to fetch you, and besieged
this city,

How many tears of remorse did you shed
   when you saw piles of Greek bodies
In heaps against these walls? Not one.
When things were going well for them,
   you conveniently remembered
   Menelaus was your husband:
His name used to spring to your lips then
   to keep Paris up to scratch.
But when the Greeks suffered any reverse,
   you forgot your first husband's name again.
Always an opportunist:
   Always keeping your eye on the main chance,
Never on virtue, never on loyalty to either.
   And of course now the Greeks have won,
You come here with some cock and bull story
   about trying to tie ropes together to make
      your escape
   and that the guards witnessed these attempt
      of yours.
You bitch, you know damn well
   all these men have been butchered
   and this because of you.
Unfortunately for you, and for me, too:
   I'm still alive.
You have one witness and this my evidence:
   How many times did I come to you
  And beg you to leave my son
  and go home to Greece?

I pleaded with you to do that,
   knowing Paris would, in time, forget you
   and marry again.
If you had gone through those walls
   the war would have stopped instantly.
And didn't I offer, again and again,
To have you conducted secretly
   back to your own people?
But you never listened, did you, my beauty?
   You didn't like the idea
Of quitting that palace where you strutted
      like a strumpet,
Where every man ogled you, including
      King Priam.
   Just look at yourself now
Decked out with Trojan jewels,
   Your vapid face thick with make-up.
The lot. And the man you're trying to
      seduce now
   Is your own husband.
You should be throwing yourself at his feet,
   wearing rags, your wig cropped,
   cringing for forgiveness.
Menelaus, be firm. Don't listen to her.
   There'll be no peace for Greece
Till she's done away with.
   Give the order, make an example of her.

CHORUS:     Your ancestors will curse you
                    If you hesitate.
                Your country will reproach you
                    if you are weak.
                Be strong, noble. Punish her.


MENELAUS:   That is my intention.
                I am convinced she left Sparta
                    Of her own free will.
                All this talk about Aphrodite
                    Is entirely irrelevant.

    [To HELEN]

                You dishonoured me:
                You shall die.
                    The army will stone you.
                You are lucky: you won't suffer for very long.
                    We endured ten years.


HELEN:      You are my husband.
                You are my King.
                    I implore you to forgive me.
                I have done nothing. No, that's not true,
                        my darling.
                    I know that I have hurt you.
                But blame the Gods for that, not me.
                    Forgive me, take me back!

HECUBA:    Let me speak now, not for my sake,
                Or Troy's sake.
            But for my enemies: the Greeks who died.
            Do not betray them.
            Do not betray their children.

MENELAUS:    Be quiet, old woman!

   [*Indicating* HELEN]

            That creature doesn't mean anything to me.

   [*To the* SOLDIERS]

            Take her aboard my ship.

HECUBA:    But only a minute ago
            You were going to have her killed immediately.

MENELAUS:    I was angry then.
            I now realize my original decision was correct.
            It is better she should die in Greece.

HECUBA:            Perhaps it is.
            But don't let her go on your boat.

MENELAUS:    Why not?

HECUBA:    Because once a man has loved,

As you have loved,
His love does not die,
    even when it seems to be dead.

MENELAUS:   That's true.
        But she whom I loved is no more.
        I never loved that
            Or if I did, it was not me.
        But I'll take your advice, old woman;
            maybe it is wise.
        She can go on some other ship,
            And when she reaches Greece
            the wretch will die as wretchedly as
                she deserves.
        I'll make an example of her:
            It's not easy to make women chaste
        But where inclination fails
            I'll make terror teach them.

    [He exits]

CHORUS:   Do you believe he will kill her?

HECUBA:   It's an even chance.

CHORUS:   Look! Look at the coward.
            What a liar he is.
        There she goes now right onto his own ship,

And he trailing behind her.
   Now the game's up.
She'll bring him to heel
And reign unpunished over Sparta.
   Nothing pays off like crime.


HECUBA:   And I thought you were just, Zeus.
   I must be going mad.
Nothing will now ever assuage
   the bitterness our dead must feel
As they, in their invisible battalions,
   crowd the beach
    to watch that brazen hussy
    step onto that ship,
Knowing they died for nothing.


CHORUS:   Absolutely nothing.
Helen will see Sparta again.
   There she will reign:
    Nothing pays off like crime.
Zeus has deprived us of everything:
   Our temples, our incensed altars;
Our city, our fertile fields, our harbours,
and you leave us with nothing, though we
    were innocent;
   while you allow Helen

To show her heels with Menelaus,
and reign over Sparta again
as if nothing had happened.
Nothing pays off like crime.
The men whom we loved,
Who fathered our children,
will haunt these blackened stones
With all the anguish of the unburied dead,
While we, their widows, wander
in far-off lands with loneliness as
our companion,
growing old, growing ugly,
and some of us becoming whores;
While that most honourable lady
calls for her golden mirror again
and sits contemplating her own smug beauty.
That's what it will be.
Nothing pays off like crime!


HECUBA: A pleasant journey, Helen.
May you drop dead on it.
If there's a God anywhere amongst all
these Gods,
May he grasp all his lightning like a dagger
and strike that ship with it.
May it catch fire, sink.
And you, Menelaus, you impotent old cuckold,

May you drown too.
I'd like the sea to swallow you both up
   then spew your swollen bodies on some beach
where your compatriots could contemplate
      your beauty:
      skin mottled and putrid,
      flesh slipping from the bone;
Then they could see:
      If crime pays off so well.

[*Enter* TALTHYBIOS *carrying the body of* ASTYANAX]

CHORUS:    Look, look, look;
      Here's the little corpse of Astyanax.
      They dropped him like a stone from a
          high tower.

TALTHYBIOS:    Hecuba, all our ships have now put to sea,
          except one,
      It waits for you and the rest of the booty.
      Achilles' son has had to leave in a hurry;
         War has started again in his country.
      A usurper has seized his father's kingdom.

HECUBA:    Ten years of it here.
      Now it starts up somewhere else again.
        Always war somewhere.
      Has his father lost his throne?

Don't expect me to be sympathetic.
And Andromeda?

TALTH:    He took her with him.
Before she left, she went and knelt by
    Hector's tomb.
I found it moving, very moving.
Neoptolemus was compassionate enough
    to allow a sepulchre to be built.
    And look at this.

HECUBA:    His shield. Hector's shield.

TALTH:    By custom, of course, it belongs
    To the son of his conqueror.
But in this instance, he's waived that right;
    So we won't be taking it with us
    To hang in the palace at Phthia.
We thought that it might distress Andromeda
    To see this relic of Hector's
    Hanging on the walls of her new
        bridal chamber.
And we didn't want to upset her.
    That would have been cruel,
And we Europeans are both civilized
    and sensitive.
So you needn't bother to try to find planks
    to make a coffin for Astyanax,

Here it is! He can rest on his father's shield.
    My instructions are
  To hand over the body to you
      since his mother has already left.
Here, take it.
    Perhaps you'll let me help you
Bury it?
    As you see, I've already cleaned it up
Or tried to; there was a lot of blood.
    Here will do, won't it?
I'll help you dig; it needn't be very deep.
    As I say, our ship's waiting.
After ten years, I can hardly believe it.


HECUBA:    Lay this shield
Upon the earth
    it protected.
      I loved him.
This ring is still polished
    where it was rubbed by his arm.
And now this eye of brass,
    which once turned back the sun,
Will lay where no light can look on it
    As a coffin for his son.

[*She takes* ASTYANAX *in her arms*]

    Bloody Greeks!

Drunk with power
  yet frightened of a child.
With Hector dead, our army slaughtered
  and our city a cinder
  you were still frightened of a child.
If you feared him, you will soon fear
    one another:
  Civil war will do to you
  what you have done to us.
And when both Troy and Greece
  have been levelled as war levels,
All that will remain
  will be this little tomb
  standing among these shattered columns.
On it, it shall bear this inscription:
  "Here lies a child
    murdered
  because he frightened Greece."

[Over the body]

    Little one,
You will never grow to strength,
  Or know that love
Which makes a man equal to a God.
  Nor will you fall or fail
As men do, from weakness or from age;
  But if men can be happy,

You could have been happy,
   All life's possibilities
Were held in this tiny hand  . . .
I always said he had his father's hands.
Now that which moved is still,
    forever still,
and the blood congeals on his battered skull.
    What waste, waste, waste.

[*To the* WOMEN]

   Go and find something
   With which we can wrap his body.

[*Some* WOMEN *go into the tent.* HECUBA *lays the corpse on the shield*]

   And to think I used to believe
     in happiness.
   I tell you destiny is drunk
     and the Gods are blind, clumsy, deaf
       and indifferent.
   A man's a fool if he thinks he's
     achieved happiness
   Unless he's on his death bed.
   Now I'll bind these wounds which will
     never heal.

[*They return*]

   Did you find anything?

A WOMAN:     Only these rags.

HECUBA:     Rags will do.
            The dead are not particular.

[*The* SOLDIERS *place the body on the shield again and
take it off.* HECUBA *watches this silently. Then she suddenly explodes with anger*]

            You filthy Gods,
        You always hated me.
            And of all cities
                Troy was the one city
                    You detested.
        Why? Didn't we mumble prayers enough?
        Make ritual and habitual sacrifice?
                And all for what?
            Today we suffer in hell.
        And you smirk at us from heaven.
            Keep your heaven!
            Go on licking your lips
        Over human misery.
            But I tell you, this time
        You omniscient immortals
            have made one small mistake:
        You should have destroyed us with
                    an earthquake
            if you wanted to sweep us out of the way.

If you'd done that
   Nobody would have ever mentioned
      Troy again.
But as it is, we held out for ten years
   against the whole of Greece,
And then were only beaten by a cheap trick.
   We die, but we do not die.
Two thousand years from now,
   our courage will still be talked about;
It was something real
   like your injustice.
You have condemned me. Now I'll
      condemn you:
   Soon all of you immortals
Will be as dead as we are!
   Come on then, what are you waiting for?
Have you run out of thunderbolts?

[Pause]

   Filthy cowards!

LEADER OF THE CHORUS:
   Don't. We beg you.
   You'll bring down other misfortunes on us.
      There's always something worse.
         Here it comes.
   Look, they're setting light to the Acropolis.

[Enter TALTHYBIOS]

TALTH: My orders were to destroy anything left standing.

[*To* AN OFFICER *of his suite*]

> Burn Troy.
> See that nothing remains.

[*To the* WOMEN]

> When you hear a trumpet,
> File down in an orderly fashion to the beach,
> It will be the signal for you to leave.

[SOLDIERS *enter*]

[*To* HECUBA]

> Ulysses has sent these men to fetch you.
> Poor old woman, you'd better follow them.


HECUBA: Now is the mountain of my misfortune capped:
> To be carried off
Leaving my Troy in flames.
> I salute those flames.
The greatest city the world has ever seen:
> To be populated by rodents,
> Decorated by brambles.
I said the Gods were deaf.
> That was not true:
They are evil.

It's a waste of time to ask them for help.
Better to rely on my legs.
Come on, old bones, don't let me down.

[*She tries to walk away*]

TALTHYBIOS:  Where's she off to? Stop her.
She must have gone out of her mind.

HECUBA:  Oh the pity of it. Poor Troy.

CHORUS:  Troy is no more. But a memory. Our memory.

HECUBA:  Oh the waste of it.
So many hands,
So many hours and hours of work.
Its glory was that it was home.
Now ash settles on what we were
And smoke describes what we've become.

CHORUS:  The pity of it.
The waste of it.

HECUBA [*Kneeling and beating the ground*]:
Oh earth, dear earth,
Be merciful.
Open up, take us into yourself.
Don't let them part us from you.

CHORUS:   What was that? That noise?

HECUBA:   That groan was the sound
              A city makes when dying.
          The walls of Troy collapse. Stand firm.
              Now make them drag us off.
          No Trojan feet will ever walk
              willingly from Troy.

[*They are all dragged off. Black out*]

[POSEIDON *appears and looks down at the prisoners waiting on the beach*]

POSEIDON:   Poor Hecuba,
              You shall not die among your enemies.
                  I shall let you go on board
              Then later take you down
                  Into my kingdom of the sea.
              And I will raise up a rock to you
                  near your native land
                  So that my waves will break over
                      you ceaselessly,
              Repeating your innumerable sorrows.

[*He turns and calls*]

              Pallas! Pallas Athene!
          Let's get to work.

[*There is a flash of lightning. Then a pause*]

Idiots!
We'll make you pay for this.
You stupid, bestial mortals
　Making war, burning cities,
　violating tombs and temples,
　torturing your enemies,
　bringing suffering on yourselves.
　　Can't you see
　　War
　　Will kill you:
　　　All of you?

**CURTAIN**

## A Note about the Author

JEAN-PAUL SARTRE, who has been ranked as a playwright of genius, was born in 1905 in Paris where he still lives and works. His first play, *The Flies* (*Les Mouches*), was produced during the German Occupation of France in spite of its underlying message of defiance. Before World War II was over, his *No Exit* (*Huis Clos*) had also been staged in Paris and brought Existentialism into the vocabularies of the world. Sartre has made living theater out of his philosophy, and his plays, in translation, have stirred intellectuals everywhere. In recent years, he has worked primarily on nonfiction. His dramatic work *The Condemned of Altona* (*Les Séquestres d'Altona*) was produced by the Repertory Theater of Lincoln Center in the 1965–6 season. *The Trojan Women* was performed at the Edinburgh Festival in the summer of 1966.

## A Note on the Type

THE TEXT of this book is set in Electra, a typeface designed by W(illiam) A(ddison) Dwiggins for the Mergenthaler Linotype Company and first made available in 1935. Electra cannot be classified as either "modern" or "old style." It is not based on any historical model, and hence does not echo any particular period or style of type design. It avoids the extreme contrast between "thick" and "thin" elements that marks most modern faces, and is without eccentricities which catch the eye and interfere with reading. In general, Electra is a simple, readable typeface which attempts to give a feeling of fluidity, power, and speed.

W. A. Dwiggins (1880–1956) was born in Martinsville, Ohio, and studied art in Chicago. In 1904 he moved to Hingham, Massachusetts, where he built a solid reputation as a designer of advertisements and as a calligrapher. He began an association with the Mergenthaler Linotype Company in 1929, and over the next twenty-seven years designed a number of book types, of which Metro, Electra, and Caledonia have been used very widely. In 1930 Dwiggins became interested in marionettes, and through the years made many important contributions to the art of puppetry and the design of marionettes.

*This book was designed by Victoria Dudley,*
*composed, printed and bound by*
*Colonial Press Inc., Clinton, Massachusetts*